TEAM SPIRIT ®

SMART BOOKS FOR YOUNG FANS

THE SAN FRANCISCO 49ERS

BY

MARK STEWART

NORWOOD HOUSE PRESS

CHICAGO, ILLINOIS

Norwood House Press
P.O. Box 316598
Chicago, Illinois 60631

For information regarding Norwood House Press, please visit our website at:
www.norwoodhousepress.com or call 866-565-2900.

All photos courtesy of Getty Images except the following:
Bowman Gum Co. (6, 34 left), Sport Magazine (7), Black Book Partners (8, 9, 10, 17, 35 bottom),
Icon SMI (14), TCMA, Ltd. (15), Topps, Inc. (20, 21, 23, 30, 31, 34 right, 37 both, 40, 41, 42 both, 45),
ESPN Magazine (22), San Francisco 49ers/NFL (28, 36, 43 bottom), Author's Collection (33),
InfoSports, Inc. (35 top left), Sports Illustrated for Kids/TIME Inc. (35 top right),
Xerographics, Inc. (43 top), Matt Richman (48).
Cover Photo: Icon SMI

The memorabilia and artifacts pictured in this book are presented for educational and informational purposes,
and come from the collection of the author.

Editor: Mike Kennedy
Designer: Ron Jaffe
Project Management: Black Book Partners, LLC.
Special thanks to Topps, Inc.

Library of Congress Cataloging-in-Publication Data

Stewart, Mark, 1960-
    The San Francisco 49ers / by Mark Stewart.
        p. cm. -- (Team spirit)
    Includes bibliographical references and index.
    Summary: "A revised Team Spirit Football edition featuring the San
Francisco 49ers that chronicles the history and accomplishments of the team.
Includes access to the Team Spirit website which provides additional
information and photos"--Provided by publisher.
    ISBN 978-1-59953-538-8 (library edition : alk. paper) -- ISBN
978-1-60357-480-8 (ebook) 1. San Francisco 49ers (Football
team)--History--Juvenile literature. I. Title. II. Title: San Francisco
Forty-niners.
    GV956.S3S84 2012
    796.332'640979461--dc23
                                              2012019095

Manufactured in the United States of America in North Mankato, Minnesota.
259R—042014

COVER PHOTO: Alex Smith throws a pass for the 49ers during a 2011 game.

Table of Contents

ABOUT OUR GLOSSARY

In this book, there may be several words that you are reading for the first time. Some are sports words, some are new vocabulary words, and some are familiar words that are used in an unusual way. All of these words are defined on page 46. Throughout the book, sports words appear in **bold type**. Regular vocabulary words appear in *bold italic type*.

Meet the 49ers

The game of football is played at a fast and furious pace. The team that moves and thinks the quickest usually comes out on top. However, it didn't used to be that way. In the early days of *professional* football, the sport was a contest of brute strength. The San Francisco 49ers were one of the teams that changed the game.

The 49ers have always looked for a different kind of player—one who combines exciting skill with great toughness. They are known as one of the most entertaining teams in all of sports. Sometimes they win and sometimes they lose, but they always play unforgettable football.

This book tells the story of the 49ers. All these years later, they still use the same recipe for success. San Francisco works hard to find special players that other teams overlook. They make the 49ers very hard to beat and San Francisco football loads of fun to watch.

Alex Smith hands off to Frank Gore. They mixed toughness with talent to become important team leaders.

Glory Days

Pro football is a sport of speed and power. It is also a sport of survival. In its first 25 years, the game survived the challenges of the *Great Depression* and *World War II*. By 1946, pro football was ready to take off. That season, a new league started play.

BUCK SHAW
San Francisco '49ers

The **All-America Football Conference (AAFC)** set itself up as a competitor to the older **National Football League (NFL)**. The AAFC placed teams in cities where the NFL did not have one, including San Francisco, California. The team was named the 49ers. It was owned by two brothers, Vic and Tony Morabito, who ran a successful lumber company. The 49ers got their name from the pioneers who traveled to California in 1849 after gold was discovered there.

The Morabitos signed a number of players who had been college stars in the San Francisco area, including quarterback Frankie Albert and receiver Alyn Beals. The Morabitos hired Buck Shaw to coach the team. He was from nearby Santa Clara College.

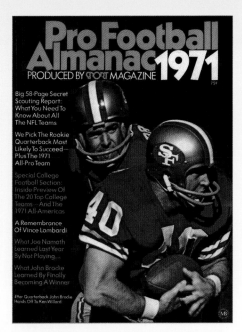

The AAFC lasted four years. The 49ers finished second in their **division** each season to the Cleveland Browns. Both teams were invited to join the NFL in 1950. Over the next few years, San Francisco put great talent on the field, including running backs Joe Perry, John Henry Johnson, and Hugh McElhenny, receivers Billy Wilson and Gordy Soltau, linemen Leo Nomellini and Bob St. Clair, and quarterback Y.A. Tittle.

After struggling in the 1960s, the 49ers regrouped and twice played for the championship of the **National Football Conference (NFC)** in the early 1970s. San Francisco had some good players, including quarterback John Brodie, receiver Gene Washington, and running back Ken Willard. Charlie Krueger, Jimmy Johnson, and Dave Wilcox led the defense.

However, it was not until Bill Walsh became the coach—and quarterback Joe Montana took control of the offense—that the 49ers turned into a great all-around team. In the 1981 season,

LEFT: Buck Shaw   **ABOVE**: John Brodie hands off to Ken Willard on the cover of a 1971 football magazine.

San Francisco won 13 games and defeated the Dallas Cowboys in the **NFC Championship Game** to reach the **Super Bowl**. Montana guided the 49ers to victory over the Cincinnati Bengals for the first championship in team history.

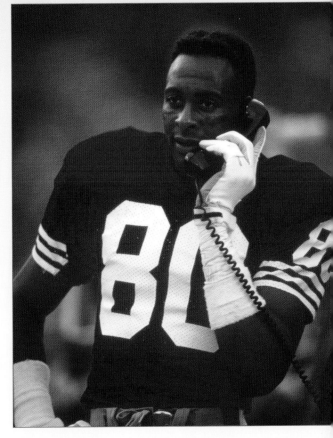

San Francisco won the Super Bowl three more times during the 1980s. The 49ers had several **All-Pro** players, including receivers Jerry Rice and Dwight Clark, running back Roger Craig, and defensive back Ronnie Lott. They got help from other stars, such as John Taylor, Keith Fahnhorst, Randy Cross, Jesse Sapolu, Keena Turner, Charles Haley, Tim McKyer, Eric Wright, and Fred Dean.

Montana was the key to San Francisco's success. He understood Walsh's offense as well as the coach did. Montana and Rice became one of the most dangerous passing duos in NFL history. Whenever the 49ers needed a big play, they came to the rescue. Both stars would end up in the **Hall of Fame**.

LEFT: Joe Montana led the 49ers to four Super Bowl championships.
ABOVE: Jerry Rice gets the latest information on a sideline telephone.

Steve Young replaced Montana as San Francisco's quarterback during the 1990s. He and Rice led the 49ers to another championship. Ricky Watters, William Floyd, and Brent Jones added to the team's offensive firepower. Ken Norton Jr., Merton Hanks, and Deion Sanders were the leaders on defense. In January of 1995, the 49ers won Super Bowl XXIX for their fifth title.

In the years that followed, the 49ers did not return to the Super Bowl, but they continued to play winning football. Young and Rice passed the torch to quarterback Jeff Garcia and receiver Terrell Owens. Charlie Garner and Garrison Hearst ranked among the NFL's best running backs. The defense welcomed young stars Bryant Young, Dana Stubblefield, and Julian Peterson.

The 49ers won the **NFC West** in 2002, but after that season, the team struggled. Over the next eight years, San Francisco had five different head coaches. None of them could find the championship *formula*, even though the 49ers had some remarkable players. Frank Gore ran for more than 1,000 yards four years in a row starting in 2006. Vernon Davis led the league in touchdown catches in 2009. Patrick Willis and Justin Smith were two of the best defensive players in the league.

What the 49ers lacked was a winning quarterback. In the 2005 **draft**, the team had picked Alex Smith. Slowly but surely, he took control of the team. At the same time, the San Francisco defense became a major force. Led by Willis, the 49ers specialized in taking the ball away from opponents with **interceptions** and **fumble** recoveries.

In 2011, the 49ers hired Jim Harbaugh to coach the team. San Francisco went 13–3 in the regular season and returned to the **playoffs** for the first time in a *decade*. Football was fun again in San Francisco, and the fans began dreaming of their next championship.

LEFT: Bryant Young made over 500 tackles for the 49ers during his career.
ABOVE: Frank Gore looks for a hole in the defense.

Home Turf

For their first 24 years, the 49ers played in Kezar Stadium. It was located in Golden Gate Park, one of San Francisco's loveliest parks. In 1971, the team moved into Candlestick Park. It was already the home of the Giants baseball team. Most fans just called it "The Stick."

In April of 2012, the 49ers launched plans for a new stadium in Santa Clara. The **blueprint** called for the stadium to be built with the surrounding land in mind. The team and its fans were very excited. Protecting the environment is important to people throughout the San Francisco area.

BY THE NUMBERS

- The 49ers' stadium has 69,732 seats.
- The stadium cost $15 million to build in the 1950s.
- The famous rock group the Beatles gave their last concert ever at the stadium in August of 1966.

A 49ers fan wears a cheese grater on his head before a home game against the Green Bay Packers, whose fans are known as "cheeseheads."

Dressed for Success

I t is hard to miss San Francisco's uniforms. The 49ers' colors are gold and a deep shade of red. They are one of the coolest-looking teams in the NFL.

The team's original colors were a brighter red and silver. The 49ers wore silver pants and red or silver helmets until 1964, when they changed to gold. In 1996, they switched to the deeper red. They also added black stripes to their jerseys.

San Francisco's *logo* was originally a California prospector, or a "49er." He was firing two pistols, and the smoke from his guns spelled out the team's name. In the 1960s, the 49ers began using a shield logo that was formed by the numbers 4 and 9. Their helmet logo, meanwhile, was an oval with *SF* inside of it. The team uses the same basic helmet logo today.

LEFT: Vernon Davis wears the team's home uniform in a 2011 game.
ABOVE: Bob St. Clair models the 49ers' uniform from the 1950s.

We Won!

When it comes to winning championships, few teams can compare to the 49ers. In 1995, San Francisco became the first team to win five Super Bowls. They all came in a span of 13 years. Before that, the team struggled to have a winning season.

The 49ers hired Bill Walsh to be their coach in 1979. In just two years, he turned them into champions. San Francisco raced through the 1981 season with a 13–3 record. In the playoffs, the 49ers won thrilling games against the New York Giants and the Dallas Cowboys to capture the NFC championship. In the Super Bowl, they faced the Cincinnati Bengals.

San Francisco fumbled the opening kickoff, but Dwight Hicks intercepted a pass to stop Cincinnati. Joe Montana took over from

LEFT: Bill Walsh gets a victory ride after Super Bowl XVI.
RIGHT: Joe Montana was the Super Bowl MVP three times.

there. He threw two touchdown passes in the first half, and Ray Wersching added a **field goal**. The Bengals fought back in the second half. With Cincinnati threatening to take the lead late in the game, the 49ers got tough, stopping the Bengals on four plays near the goal line. The final score was 26–21. Montana was named the game's **Most Valuable Player (MVP)**.

Montana was also the star during San Francisco's next trip to the Super Bowl, in 1985. This time, the 49ers played the Miami Dolphins. In a battle between two great quarterbacks, Montana got the better of Dan Marino, and the 49ers won 38–16. The Dolphins were ahead 10–7 in the second quarter, but Roger Craig scored two touchdowns and Montana ran for another to break the game open. Montana passed for 331 yards, three touchdowns, and once again was named MVP.

Montana's greatest championship moment came in Super Bowl XXIII, in 1989. The 49ers faced the Bengals again. This time, San Francisco trailed 16–13 with just over three minutes left. That's when Montana went to work. Starting from his own 8-yard line, he drove his team nearly the entire length of the field. He relied heavily on Jerry Rice, a young star who had become his favorite receiver. Then, with the Bengals expecting another pass to Rice, Montana threw a perfect spiral to John Taylor in the end zone to win the game 20–16. Rice, who caught 11 passes, was named MVP.

One year later, San Francisco won its fourth title. Walsh was no longer calling the shots on the sideline. He had retired, and George Seifert was now in charge. The 49ers kept rolling.

In Super Bowl XXIV against the Denver Broncos, San Francisco was almost unstoppable. Montana threw five touchdown passes.

Rice caught three of them. The 49ers also scored three touchdowns on the ground, including a pair by Tom Rathman. The San Francisco defense was just as impressive, and the 49ers won, 55–10. Montana took his third MVP award.

The 49ers' fifth Super Bowl victory came against the San Diego Chargers, in 1995. Steve Young was now San Francisco's quarterback. He had backed up Montana

for five years before getting his chance to start. On the third play of the game, Young connected on a beautiful pass to Rice, who outran the defense for a 44-yard touchdown.

The 49ers never looked back. Rice scored twice more, and running back Ricky Watters added a pair of touchdowns on the way to a 49–26 victory. Young set a Super Bowl record with six touchdown passes and was named the game's MVP.

LEFT: Jerry Rice scores a touchdown in Super Bowl XXIII.
ABOVE: Rice and Steve Young celebrate their victory over the San Diego Chargers.

Go-To Guys

T o be a true star in the NFL, you need more than fast feet and a big body. You have to be a "go-to guy"—someone the coach wants on the field at the end of a big game. 49ers fans have had a lot to cheer about over the years, including these great stars …

THE PIONEERS

JOE PERRY   Running Back

• BORN: 1/22/1927 • DIED: 4/25/2011 • PLAYED FOR TEAM: 1948 TO 1960 & 1963

Joe Perry was nicknamed the "Jet" because he could sprint through the smallest openings. He was especially good on short **screen passes**. In 1953 and 1954, Perry became the first runner in history with back-to-back 1,000-yard seasons.

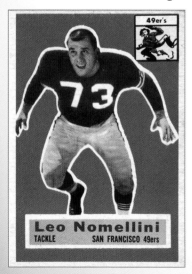

Leo Nomellini
TACKLE   SAN FRANCISCO 49ers

LEO NOMELLINI   Lineman

• BORN: 6/19/1924   • DIED: 10/17/2000

• PLAYED FOR TEAM: 1950 TO 1963

Leo Nomellini was one of the toughest linemen of the 1950s. He played both offense and defense and was an All-Pro on both sides of the ball. Nomellini did not miss a game in 14 seasons.

HUGH McELHENNY   Running Back

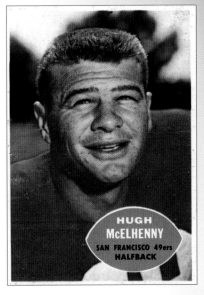

- BORN: 12/31/1928   • PLAYED FOR TEAM: 1952 TO 1960

Hugh McElhenny was nicknamed the "King." No runner during the 1950s was more exciting to watch. Once McElhenny passed the line of scrimmage, he made moves that left tacklers grabbing at air.

BOB ST. CLAIR   Offensive Lineman

- BORN: 2/18/1931   • PLAYED FOR TEAM: 1953 TO 1963

Few players were scarier than Bob St. Clair. He stood 6′ 9″ and was a powerful blocker—and also liked to eat raw meat! The 49ers often put him in on defense if they needed to block a field goal.

JOHN BRODIE   Quarterback

- BORN: 8/14/1935   • PLAYED FOR TEAM: 1957 TO 1973

John Brodie might have been the most talented passer in the NFL when he played for the 49ers. His athletic ability stretched beyond the football field. After he retired, Brodie became a professional golfer.

KEN WILLARD   Running Back

- BORN: 7/14/1943   • PLAYED FOR TEAM: 1965 TO 1973

The 49ers were a good passing team in the 1960s and early 1970s. That was because opponents usually focused on stopping running back Ken Willard. He played in the **Pro Bowl** four times in his first five seasons.

LEFT: Leo Nomellini   **ABOVE**: Hugh McElhenny

JOE MONTANA   Quarterback

• BORN: 6/11/1956   • PLAYED FOR TEAM: 1979 TO 1992

Joe Montana was not built like an NFL superstar, but he was one of the smartest and bravest men who ever took the field. He led the NFC in passing five times and guided the 49ers to more than two dozen fourth-quarter comebacks during his career.

RONNIE LOTT   Defensive Back

• BORN: 5/8/1959   • PLAYED FOR TEAM: 1981 TO 1990

No one tackled harder than Ronnie Lott. He was at his best when he played safety and was free to roam the field. Lott was an All-Pro five times.

JERRY RICE   Receiver

• BORN: 10/13/1962   • PLAYED FOR TEAM: 1985 TO 2000

When Jerry Rice caught a pass, the play was just beginning. The speedy receiver could snatch a ball on the run and quickly shift into an even faster gear. Rice scored 186 touchdowns for the 49ers.

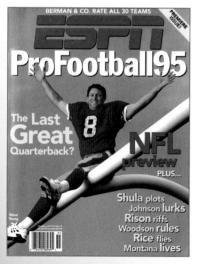

STEVE YOUNG   Quarterback

• BORN: 10/11/1961   • PLAYED FOR TEAM: 1987 TO 1999

Steve Young was one of the best athletes in league history. He led the NFL in touchdown passes four times and was the top-rated quarterback six times. Young was voted the league MVP twice.

ALEX SMITH Quarterback

- BORN: 5/7/1984   • FIRST YEAR WITH TEAM: 2005

As a young NFL quarterback, Alex Smith had his ups and downs for the 49ers. In 2011, he came into his own and was one of the top-rated passers in the league. That season, Smith showed great *poise* under pressure in leading San Francisco to the NFC Championship Game.

FRANK GORE Running Back

- BORN: 5/14/1983   • FIRST YEAR WITH TEAM: 2005

Frank Gore reminded many San Francisco fans of Joe Perry. Gore could blast through tiny holes in the defense, and then use his explosive speed to make big gains. He rushed for more than 1,000 yards five times from 2006 to 2011.

PATRICK WILLIS Linebacker

- BORN: 1/25/1985   • FIRST YEAR WITH TEAM: 2007

Patrick Willis was big, fast, and strong. When he joined the 49ers, he worked with assistant coach Mike Singletary to become one of the top linebackers in the NFL. He was voted the Defensive **Rookie** of the Year in 2007.

LEFT: Steve Young poses for a 1995 magazine cover.
ABOVE: Alex Smith and Frank Gore share space on a Topps trading card.

Calling the Shots

A team with great talent does not always win a championship. The players need a great coach to lead them. In the 1940s and 1950s—and again in the 1970s—the 49ers came very close to winning a title. The team had a good coach in each decade—Buck Shaw, Frankie Albert, and Dick Nolan—but none of them could find the final piece in the championship puzzle.

That changed after the 49ers hired Bill Walsh. From 1968 to 1975, Walsh had worked for the Cincinnati Bengal as an assistant to Paul Brown, one the NFL's greatest coaches ever. He learned a lot from Brown. Walsh came to believe that an offense that used short, accurate passes to its receivers and running backs could gain an advantage over opponents. As head coach of the 49ers, Walsh decided to put this plan to work.

First, he had to rebuild the team from the bottom up. Walsh looked for players who could fit into his offense and improve his defense. Thanks to young stars such as Joe Montana, Dwight Clark, and Ronnie Lott, the 49ers became championship *contenders*— and stayed at or near the top of the NFL for 20 seasons.

George Seifert and Bill Walsh swap stories about coaching the 49ers.

The coach who followed Walsh was George Seifert. Needless to say, nothing less than a championship would be acceptable. Under this great pressure, Seifert led the 49ers to the Super Bowl in his first season. Even as Walsh's players left the team, Seifert continued to win. He guided the 49ers to the NFC Championship Game three more times and led them to another Super Bowl victory.

In recent years, the 49ers have continued to find great coaching talent. Steve Mariucci led the team to the playoffs four times. Mike Singletary turned the team's defense into an awesome weapon. In 2011, the 49ers looked for a new spark. They hired Jim Harbaugh, and he took them back to the NFC Championship Game in his first season on the sidelines.

One Great Day

When the 49ers took the field against the Dallas Cowboys to decide the champion of the NFC for 1981, there was more at stake than just a trip to the Super Bowl. San Francisco fans hoped to *avenge* three heartbreaking losses to Dallas during the 1970s. The teams had met in the playoffs in 1970, 1971, and 1972. Each time, the Cowboys won. Now it was time for "payback."

The 49ers scored first when Joe Montana hit Freddie Solomon with a short touchdown pass. The Cowboys came back to take a 10–7 lead. The game seesawed back and forth all afternoon. Dwight Clark caught a 20-yard touchdown pass to put the 49ers ahead, but Dallas scored again before halftime to go ahead 17–14. San Francisco reached the end zone in the third quarter to make the score 21–17. Dallas responded with 10 points in the fourth quarter to lead 27–21.

The experienced Cowboys rarely lost in these situations. However, they had never faced Montana. "Joe Cool" led the 49ers

Dwight Clark leaps high to make "The Catch."

from his own 11-yard line deep into Dallas territory with a minute left. Montana called a pass play on third down. When the Cowboys chased him toward the right sideline, he looked for an open teammate.

At the very last instant, Montana floated the ball toward the back of the end zone. He was throwing to a spot that only he and Clark knew about. They had run this "blind" play in practice many times and saved it just for these situations. Clark leapt high and snared the ball, landing with both feet inbounds.

Forever after, this play would be known as "The Catch." Ray Wersching's extra point gave San Francisco a 28–27 victory. It signaled the end of the Dallas *dynasty* and the beginning of the 49ers' glory years.

Legend Has It

Was Dwight Clark the first choice for Joe Montana on "The Catch?"

LEGEND HAS IT that he was not. Freddie Solomon was the primary receiver on the play that won the NFC championship for the 49ers. That means he was the first player that Montana looked for after the ball was snapped. Solomon was a good choice. He was San Francisco's fastest receiver. However, Solomon slipped while running his pass route. When Montana was forced to scramble, he threw to Clark instead. It may have been the luckiest slip in NFL history!

ABOVE: Freddie Solomon

LEGEND HAS IT that Hardy Brown was. Brown was a linebacker for the 49ers from 1951 to 1955. Though he was small and slow, he hit opponents with such tremendous force that they often had to be carried off the field. Brown would crouch just before tackling the ball carrier, and then "spring" into the player's upper body, using his shoulder as a battering ram. He was at his best covering punts and kickoffs. "Ball carriers avoided him like the *plague*," teammate Gordy Soltau once said. "He was something!"

Which San Francisco coach also worked as a hotel bellhop?

LEGEND HAS IT that Bill Walsh did. Prior to Super Bowl XVI, Walsh wanted to ease the tension that his players were feeling. He decided to play a joke on them. Walsh disguised himself as a bellhop at the team's hotel. As the 49ers stepped off the team bus, he greeted them and offered to help with their luggage. The prank worked. San Francisco beat the Cincinnati Bengals 26–21.

The 1980s and 1990s were wonderful times for fans of the 49ers. The decade that followed was not so great. From 2004 to 2010, the team did not have a single winning season. Rebuilding the club proved difficult. As the 2011 season began, the 49ers

49ERS
ALEX SMITH

started all over again with a new coach. His name was Jim Harbaugh. No one was more focused on winning.

Harbaugh got the 49ers off to a good start. They won their opening game and barely lost their next one in **overtime**. After that, San Francisco was almost unbeatable. The defense was fantastic, and the offense made big plays all season long. The 49ers finished the year at 13–3!

The team's biggest test came at home in the playoffs against the New Orleans Saints. Almost every

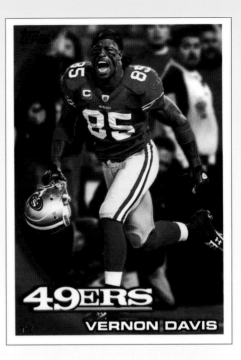

LEFT: Alex Smith
RIGHT: Vernon Davis

expert believed the Saints would win the Super Bowl. The 49ers had other plans. They led 23–17 with four minutes left. However, the game was far from over.

The Saints regained the lead on a long touchdown play. Two minutes later, Alex Smith made a desperate 28-yard touchdown run to give the 49ers a 29–24 lead. New Orleans came right back with less than two minutes remaining. Drew Brees fired a scoring pass to Jimmy Graham, and the Saints were back on top, 32–29.

The 49ers got the ball back on their own 15-yard line with 94 seconds left. Smith calmly moved the team down the field. With time running out, he threw a pass to Vernon Davis, who caught the ball near the goal line with the defense waiting for him. Davis powered into the end zone for the winning touchdown. The 49ers earned the victory in one of the wildest games in NFL history, 36–32.

Team Spirit

The 49ers hold a special place in the hearts of San Francisco residents. That's because they are the city's oldest major professional sports team. The 49ers draw fans from all over northern California. Many families have been attending games for more than 50 years.

During games, the Gold Rush cheerleaders entertain the fans. They have been performing since 1983 and were one of the first dance teams in the NFL. Also roaming the sidelines for the 49ers is their team *mascot*, Sourdough Sam. San Francisco is famous for its sourdough bread, which is how this 1849-style gold miner got his nickname.

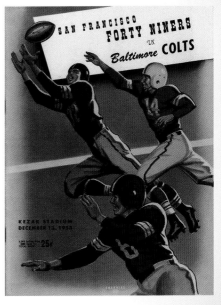

Prior to kickoff in San Francisco, thousands of fans hold tailgate parties. That *tradition* showed no signs of ending as the team planned to open a new stadium. In fact, the 49ers designed the new complex with these fun parking lot parties in mind.

LEFT: San Francisco fans aren't afraid to toot their own horns.
ABOVE: Fans bought this program for a 1953 game between the 49ers and the Baltimore Colts.

Timeline

In this timeline, each Super Bowl is listed under the year it was played. Remember that the Super Bowl is held early in the year and is actually part of the previous season. For example, Super Bowl XLVI was played on February 5, 2012, but it was the championship of the 2011 NFL season.

1946
The 49ers finish 9–5 in their first season.

1982
The 49ers win Super Bowl XVI for their first championship.

1954
Joe Perry leads the NFL in rushing for the second year in a row.

1962
Abe Woodson is the NFL's top kickoff returner for the third year in a row.

1970
Gene Washington leads the NFL with 1,100 receiving yards.

Quarterback Frankie Albert led the 49ers in their first season.

Abe Woodson

ABE WOODSON
HALFBACK   SAN FRANCISCO 49'ERS

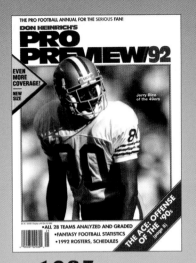

Jerry
Rice

Terrell
Owens

1987

Jerry Rice sets an NFL record with 22 touchdown receptions.

2001

Terrell Owens leads the NFL in touchdown catches.

2006

Frank Gore sets a team record with 1,695 rushing yards.

1992

Steve Young is named NFL MVP.

1995

The 49ers win their fifth championship.

2012

The 49ers return to the NFC Championship Game.

Steve
Young

Fun Facts

BACK FROM THE BRINK

In a 2003 playoff game against the New York Giants, the 49ers trailed 38–14 in the third quarter. San Francisco scored 25 points to win 39–38. It was the second-greatest comeback in playoff history.

ROOKIE SENSATION

In 1980, Earl Cooper was the team's first pick in the draft. It was a smart choice. That season, Cooper finished first in the NFC with 83 pass receptions.

JOE COMEBACK

In a 1980 game against the New Orleans Saints, Joe Montana led the 49ers to victory after trailing 35–7. It was the first of 26 fourth-quarter comebacks for Montana during his career with San Francisco.

ABOVE: Earl Cooper
RIGHT: Y.A. Tittle and R.C. Owens perfected the Alley-Oop pass.

ALLEY-OOP

The most famous pass play of the 1950s was the 49ers' "Alley-Oop." Y.A. Tittle would throw a high pass to teammate R.C. Owens, a former basketball star who was the best jumper in the NFL. He would soar a foot above the defensive players to catch the ball.

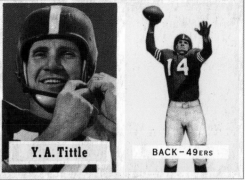

Y. A. Tittle   BACK–49ERS

HARD MEN TO BLOCK

The NFL did not keep official records for **sacks** in the 1970s, but the 49ers did. Their "sack-master" was linebacker Cedric Hardman. From 1970 to 1979, he had 120 sacks. Fred Dean gave Hardman a run for his money. Dean was a pass-rushing specialist for the 49ers from 1981 to 1985. He once had six sacks in a game.

R. C. OWENS
END-HALFBACK   SAN FRANCISCO 49'ERS

MAD HOPS

The fastest 49er in history may have been Renaldo "Skeets" Nehemiah. The former track star owned many world records in the hurdles when he joined the team in 1982.

Talking Football

"Joe is the man!"

▶ **Jerry Rice**, *on Joe Montana*

"We had a lot of warriors on our team. We didn't care about winning. We cared about perfection."

▶ **Ronnie Lott**, *on the San Francisco teams of the 1980s*

"As a quarterback, you have to be cool and **contained**."

▶ **John Brodie**, *on being the leader of an NFL team*

"I don't take vacations."

▶ **Jim Harbaugh**, *on his intense desire to win*

"Jerry taught me a lot on and off the field."

▶ **Terrell Owens**, *on Jerry Rice*

"We felt like no one could stop us when we got in that rhythm."

▶ **Frank Gore**, *on the timing between him and his blockers*

"What I do best is not let people block me. I just hate to be blocked."

▶ **Dave Wilcox**, *on what made him an All-Pro linebacker*

"Fear can be conquered. I became a better player when I learned that lesson."

▶ **Roger Craig**, *on what it takes to be an NFL star*

LEFT: Ronnie Lott
ABOVE: Terrell Owens and Jerry Rice

Great Debates

People who root for the 49ers love to compare their favorite moments, teams, and players. Some debates have been going on for years! How would you settle these classic football arguments?

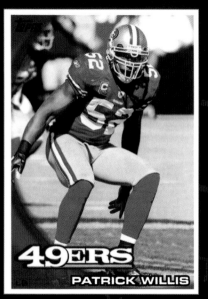

PATRICK WILLIS

Patrick Willis was San Francisco's greatest linebacker ...

... because after joining the 49ers in 2007, he quickly became the leader of their defense. Willis (LEFT) was honored as an All-Pro as a rookie, when he led the NFL in tackles. He was an All-Pro three more times from 2009 to 2011. Ray Lewis, one of the greatest linebackers ever, said of Willis, "He reminds me of myself—a lot, a lot, a lot."

Hang on a minute. Don't count out Dave Wilcox ...

... because he was one of the top linebackers of his day. Wilcox earned All-Pro honors four times in the 1960s and 1970s. He was almost impossible to block, and no one tackled as hard as he did. Wilcox was especially good at covering tight ends. Fans called him the "Intimidator."

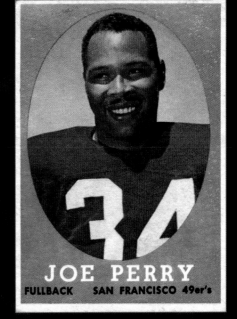

JOE PERRY
FULLBACK   SAN FRANCISCO 49er's

... because no team has ever had three Hall of Famers playing together at the same time. From 1954 to 1957, Hugh McElhenny, Joe Perry (RIGHT), and John Henry Johnson lined up behind Hall of Fame quarterback Y.A. Tittle. Fans called it the "Million Dollar Backfield." The three backs were perfectly matched. McElhenny had great moves and balance, Perry had blinding speed, and Johnson was a powerful runner who loved to block as much as he loved to carry the ball.

The runners of the 1980s were even better ....

... because they did something the Million Dollar Backfield couldn't—win championships. Roger Craig, Wendell Tyler, and Tom Rathman were tough, steady backs who picked up important yards against the NFL's best defenses. Craig, in particular, is often overlooked because he played with Joe Montana and Jerry Rice. In eight seasons with the 49ers, he gained more than 11,000 rushing and receiving yards and scored 87 touchdowns.

For the Record

The great 49ers teams and players have left their marks on the record books. These are the "best of the best" …

BILLY WILSON
END   SAN FRANCISCO 49'ERS

Billy Wilson

Roger Craig

49ERS AWARD WINNERS

WINNER	AWARD	YEAR
Billy Wilson	Pro Bowl MVP	1955
Hugh McElhenny	Pro Bowl Offensive MVP	1958
John Brodie	Most Valuable Player	1970
Bruce Taylor	Defensive Rookie of the Year	1970
Bill Walsh	Coach of the Year	1981
Joe Montana	Super Bowl XVI MVP	1982
Joe Montana	Super Bowl XIX MVP	1985
Jerry Rice	Offensive Player of the Year	1987
Roger Craig	Offensive Player of the Year	1988
Joe Montana	Offensive Player of the Year	1989
Joe Montana	Most Valuable Player	1989
Jerry Rice	Super Bowl XXIII MVP	1989
Joe Montana	Most Valuable Player	1990
Joe Montana	Super Bowl XXIV MVP	1990
Steve Young	Offensive Player of the Year	1992
Steve Young	Most Valuable Player	1992
Dana Stubblefield	Defensive Rookie of the Year	1993
Jerry Rice	Offensive Player of the Year	1993
Deion Sanders	Defensive Player of the Year	1994
Steve Young	Most Valuable Player	1994
Steve Young	Super Bowl XXIX MVP	1995
Jerry Rice	Pro Bowl MVP	1996
Dana Stubblefield	Defensive Player of the Year	1997
Bryant Young	Comeback Player of the Year	1999
Garrison Hearst	Comeback Player of the Year	2001
Jim Harbaugh	Coach of the Year	2011

49ERS ACHIEVEMENTS

ACHIEVEMENT	YEAR
NFC West Champions	1970
NFC West Champions	1971
NFC West Champions	1972
NFC West Champions	1981
NFC Champions	1981
Super Bowl XVI Champions	1981*
NFC West Champions	1983
NFC West Champions	1984
NFC Champions	1984
Super Bowl XIX Champions	1984*
NFC West Champions	1986
NFC West Champions	1987
NFC West Champions	1988
NFC Champions	1988
Super Bowl XXIII Champions	1988*
NFC West Champions	1989
NFC Champions	1989
Super Bowl XXIV Champions	1989*
NFC West Champions	1990
NFC West Champions	1992
NFC West Champions	1993
NFC West Champions	1994
NFC Champions	1994
Super Bowl XXIX Champions	1994*
NFC West Champions	1995
NFC West Champions	1997
NFC West Champions	2002
NFC West Champions	2011

Super Bowls are played early the following year, but the game is counted as the championship of this season.

ABOVE: Dave Wilcox was the team's top linebacker in the early 1970s.
BELOW: Fred Dean was a pass-rushing star during the 1980s.

Pinpoints

The history of a football team is made up of many smaller stories. These stories take place all over the map—not just in the city a team calls "home." Match the pushpins on these maps to the **Team Facts**, and you will begin to see the story of the 49ers unfold!

TEAM FACTS

1 San Francisco, California—*The 49ers have played here since 1946.*

2 Los Angeles, California—*Bill Walsh was born here.*

3 Seattle, Washington—*Alex Smith was born here.*

4 Albuquerque, New Mexico—*Ronnie Lott was born here.*

5 Davenport, Iowa—*Roger Craig was born here.*

6 Crawford, Mississippi—*Jerry Rice was born here.*

7 New Orleans, Louisiana—*The 49ers won their first championship here.*

8 New Eagle, Pennsylvania—*Joe Montana was born here.*

9 Richmond, Virginia—*Ken Willard was born here.*

10 Miami, Florida—*The 49ers won their fifth championship here.*

11 Laie, Western Samoa—*Jesse Sapolu was born here.*

12 Lucca, Italy—*Leo Nomellini was born here.*

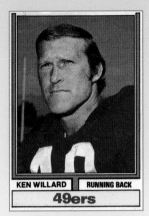

KEN WILLARD — RUNNING BACK
49ers

Ken Willard

45

Glossary

🏈 Football Words
🧠 Vocabulary Words

🏈 **ALL-AMERICA FOOTBALL CONFERENCE (AAFC)**—The professional league that played for four seasons, from 1946 to 1949.

🏈 **ALL-PRO**—An honor given to the best players at their positions at the end of each season.

🧠 *AVENGE*—Punish for a past insult or defeat.

🧠 *BLUEPRINT*—A detailed plan used to build something.

🧠 *CONTAINED*—In control of one's emotions.

🧠 *CONTENDERS*—People or teams that compete for a championship.

🧠 *DECADE*—A period of 10 years; also specific periods, such as the 1950s.

🏈 **DIVISION**—A group of teams that play in the same part of the country.

🏈 **DRAFT**—The annual meeting during which NFL teams choose from a group of the best college players.

🧠 *DYNASTY*—A family, group, or team that maintains power over time.

🏈 **FIELD GOAL**—A goal from the field, kicked over the crossbar and between the goal posts. A field goal is worth three points.

🧠 *FORMULA*—A set way of doing something.

🏈 **FUMBLE**—A ball that is dropped by the player carrying it.

🧠 *GREAT DEPRESSION*—The economic crisis that started in 1929 and lasted until the 1940s.

🏈 **HALL OF FAME**—The museum in Canton, Ohio, where football's greatest players are honored. A player voted into the Hall of Fame is sometimes called a "Hall of Famer."

🏈 **INTERCEPTIONS**—Passes that are caught by the defensive team.

🧠 *LOGO*—A symbol or design that represents a company or team.

🧠 *MASCOT*—An animal or person believed to bring a group good luck.

🏈 **MOST VALUABLE PLAYER (MVP)**—The award given each year to the league's best player; also given to the best player in the Super Bowl and Pro Bowl.

🏈 **NATIONAL FOOTBALL CONFERENCE (NFC)**—One of two groups of teams that make up the NFL.

🏈 **NATIONAL FOOTBALL LEAGUE (NFL)**—The league that started in 1920 and is still operating today.

🏈 **NFC CHAMPIONSHIP GAME**—The game played to determine which NFC team will go to the Super Bowl.

🏈 **NFC WEST**—A division for teams that play in the western part of the country.

🏈 **OVERTIME**—The extra period played when a game is tied after 60 minutes.

🧠 *PLAGUE*—A deadly disease.

🏈 **PLAYOFFS**—The games played after the regular season to determine which teams play in the Super Bowl.

🧠 *POISE*—Calmness and confidence.

🏈 **PRO BOWL**—The NFL's all-star game, played after the regular season.

🧠 *PROFESSIONAL*—Paid to play.

🏈 **ROOKIE**—A player in his first season.

🏈 **SACKS**—Tackles of the quarterback behind the line of scrimmage.

🏈 **SCREEN PASSES**—Short passes thrown to a player with a protective "screen" of blockers in front of him.

🏈 **SUPER BOWL**—The championship of the NFL, played between the winners of the National Football Conference and American Football Conference.

🧠 *TRADITION*—A belief or custom that is handed down from generation to generation.

🧠 *WORLD WAR II*—The war among the major powers of Europe, Asia, and North America that lasted from 1939 to 1945. The United States entered the war in 1941.

OVERTIME

TEAM SPIRIT introduces a great way to stay up to date with your team! Visit our **OVERTIME** link and get connected to the latest and greatest updates. **OVERTIME** serves as a young reader's ticket to an exclusive web page—with more stories, fun facts, team records, and photos of the 49ers. Content is updated during and after each season. The **OVERTIME** feature also enables readers to send comments and letters to the author! Log onto:

www.norwoodhousepress.com/library.aspx
and click on the tab: **TEAM SPIRIT** to access **OVERTIME**.

Read all the books in the series to learn more about professional sports. For a complete listing of the baseball, basketball, football, and hockey teams in the **TEAM SPIRIT** series, visit our website at:

www.norwoodhousepress.com/library.aspx

On the Road

SAN FRANCISCO 49ERS
490 Jamestown Avenue
San Francisco, California 94124
408-562-4949
www.49ers.com

THE PRO FOOTBALL HALL OF FAME
2121 George Halas Drive NW
Canton, Ohio 44708
330-456-8207
www.profootballhof.com

On the Bookshelf

To learn more about the sport of football, look for these books at your library or bookstore:

- Frederick, Shane. *The Best of Everything Football Book.* North Mankato, Minnesota: Capstone Press, 2011.

- Jacobs, Greg. *The Everything Kids' Football Book: The All-Time Greats, Legendary Teams, Today's Superstars—And Tips on Playing Like a Pro.* Avon, Massachusetts: Adams Media Corporation, 2010.

- Editors of *Sports Illustrated for Kids. 1st and 10: Top 10 Lists of Everything in Football.* New York, New York: Sports Illustrated Books, 2011.

Index

PAGE NUMBERS IN **BOLD** REFER TO ILLUSTRATIONS.

About the Author

MARK STEWART has written more than 50 books on football and over 150 sports books for kids. He grew up in New York City during the 1960s rooting for the Giants and Jets, and was lucky enough to meet players from both teams. Mark comes from a family of writers. His grandfather was Sunday Editor of *The New York Times,* and his mother was Articles Editor of *Ladies' Home Journal* and *McCall's.* Mark has profiled hundreds of athletes over the past 25 years. He has also written several books about his native New York and New Jersey, his home today. Mark is a graduate of Duke University, with a degree in history. He lives and works in a home overlooking Sandy Hook, New Jersey. You can contact Mark through the Norwood House Press website.